Also by Stu Cranstence

MY Findings Volume II:
Return of the Saguaros

MY Findings

by Stu Cranstence

You can find more info about Stu Cranstence by visiting
http://rhodesandrose.com/?cat=46
Videos of Stu out in the field are also available at
www.youtube.com/user/doctorodub

Photos by Ron Cranstence
Cover design by RonCranstence
Book design by Ron Cranstence

ISBN 978-1-7325402-1-7

Hardy Perennial Press LLC
1645 W. Valencia rd #109-154
Tucson AZ 85746

My brother Ron Cranstence contributed - in his way- to this book.
Although the important work like collecting findings and speculating
on them was done by me, the lesser tasks such as photography, typing,
layout, storage of findings, transportation, sanitation and financing
were handled by Ron. I suppose I should thank Ron for enabling me to
do all the things I do.

Stu Cranstence

Contents

Introduction

When I am in the field I make many significant findings. By using techniques such as observication and geoligication, and tools like pointer sticks and my brother Ron, I am able to clear up the misconceptions of the normal person and allow them to see how things actually are. Most people know nearly nothing, so this book will remove the cloak of ignorance worn by you, the reader.

Chapter 1 - My Methods

a. When Nature Calls

Probably the most unpleasant time is when nature calls. If you don't know what I'm talking about, I will give you a hint - it's called "number two". When out in the field, after three or four days, I have to make a choice - either go home or do number two in the field. When I make choice number two, it's very important that I cover it with a pile of rocks so that I don't accidentally step in it later. The times that I have neglected this simple step, I have regretted it later and I end up losing my temper.

Above - Types of POINTER STICKS
From left to right: Small POINTER STICK, Medium Small POINTER STICK, Medium POINTER STICK, Medium Bent POINTER STICK, Medium Large POINTER STICK, Extra-Medium Large POINTER STICK, Large POINTER STICK, Extra Large POINTER STICK.

b. Pointer Sticks

POINTER STICKS are perhaps my most important tool and I enjoy using them very much. They allow me to indicate precisely where everyone should look while I am talking. And, most impressively, I make sure to have a wide variety of POINTER STICK lengths. That way, if what I am talking about is far away, by using one of my very long POINTER STICKS, I never have to get up or stop talking.

Correct use of POINTER STICK(Medium Large)

c. Old Trusty

In life, no one can be trusted and everyone seems to irritate me. That's why I always make sure to have my cooler close by my side. There's nothing more reassuring than a full cooler - its sight, its feel, its weight, the soft thud sound it makes when I pat it. And, just as surely, the thought of being in the field without Old Trusty has tormented me for many a sleepless night. Can you imagine what it would be like to be in the field and realize your brother had forgot to bring the cooler and a backup supply? He would have to turn right around to correct the situation and it would be very hard on me.

Chapter 2 - Wind

Wind has been around for a long time. It was invented by the ANCIENT EGYPTIANS over a hundred years ago. Back then no one spoke english, they only spoke CHINESE. That's why they call it wind because it's an ancient Chinese word that means "wind".

Wind is created by WIND MILLS. These 'Mills of Wind' spin around and around until wind comes flying out. I have seen these WIND MILLS as I drive around looking for findings. How did they get there? How long does it take for them to grow to such heights? What is their purpose? No one knows.

It is my contention that people should begin to study WIND. Someday, I believe man will be able to HARNESS THE POWER OF THE WIND. Imagine a day when WIND is converted to gasoline - gasoline that can power more WIND MILLS to create more WIND to convert into gasoline. Fantasy?

Well, was Einstein fantasizing when he invented gravity?

I rest my case.

Above - mills of wind.

Chapter 3 - Women Scientists

Have you ever wondered why there are no WOMEN SCIENTISTS? The reasons are too numerous to fit into this one volume. And yet, I believe that one day, in EONS HENCE, women will be allowed, slowly at first, to assist in scientist's most basic findings. Reckless? Perhaps. Imagine the nagging - day and night, night and day! But times change. And I believe now is the time for me to consider allowing women to become scientists.

Yes. Women should be allowed to enter the world of science. And I say, its about time!

Chapter 4 - Fast Growing Mushrooms

Few things bring me more pleasure than the discovery of a large FAST GROWING MUSHROOM. One day an area will have no FAST GROWING MUSHROOMS and the next day that same area will be covered with them. Fascinating! After years of honing my senses I am now able to find these FAST GROWING MUSHROOMS in ever larger quantities. Most people don't even know what they are! Luckily, I do. And so I gather these WONDERS OF NATURE and put them in boxes or trash bags so that they can be brought to my brother, Ron. Since I have done all the work, Ron needs only to sort through them and find a place to keep them. By doing his small part, Ron enables me to continue in all the work I do. And Ron gets to feel like he is worthwhile. I don't need his thanks. The joy of discovery is all the thanks I need.

Chapter 5 - Darwin

Darwin (no one knows his last name) is one of the most famous scientists of all time, which is why he is so great.
The most famous event of Darwin's career happened when he was out looking around for the MISSING LINK. He looked over there and he couldn't believe what he saw. There were several figures standing in a line. The first figure was a monkey, all bent over. The next in line was a monkey too, but he didn't bend over as much. Next in line came another monkey who didn't have as much hair and stood up straighter than the others. The next figure stood up pretty straight and looked like a man who was very hairy. The last in line was a man. But the disgusting thing was that this man was nude! One of his legs was stepping forward and this leg blocked your view of his, 'you know what'. Even if you held the picture at an angle and looked very hard, you couldn't see anything. All of a sudden, a giant boulder came rolling towards Darwin and he had to run for his life or he would be trapped in the cave. But at the last minute he found the MISSING LINK! It was made of solid gold and it was shaped like a skull! He had found the MISSING LINK and was now the most famous scientist in the world!

The lake waters become rough due to the smooth rocks.

Above and below - examples of smooth rocks

Chapter 6 - The Great Pacific Lake

I'll never forget the day I discovered THE GREAT PACIFIC LAKE. I was just driving along and there it was! To get a sense of just how big it really is, imagine a lake the size of a parking lot! There are no living things in or around THE GREAT PACIFIC LAKE. Rocks may be seen there but they died over a hundred years ago when the ANCIENT CHINESE were building the lake. Some of these rocks are very smooth. They are called SMOOTH ROCKS and they cause the waters of the lake to become quite rough.

After a few minutes I completed my observications of THE GREAT PACIFIC LAKE. Having learned all there is to know about it there is no need for me to ever go back to this 'MYSTERY OF THE DEEP.'

Reference stick

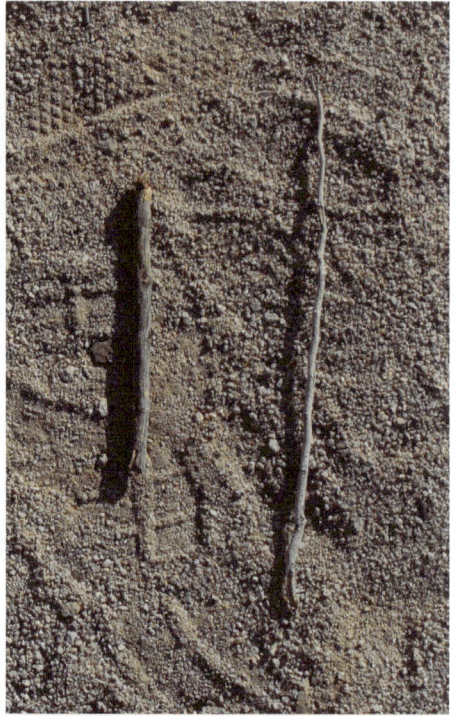
BONESTICK Date - ? Location - ?

BONESTICK Date - ? Location - ?

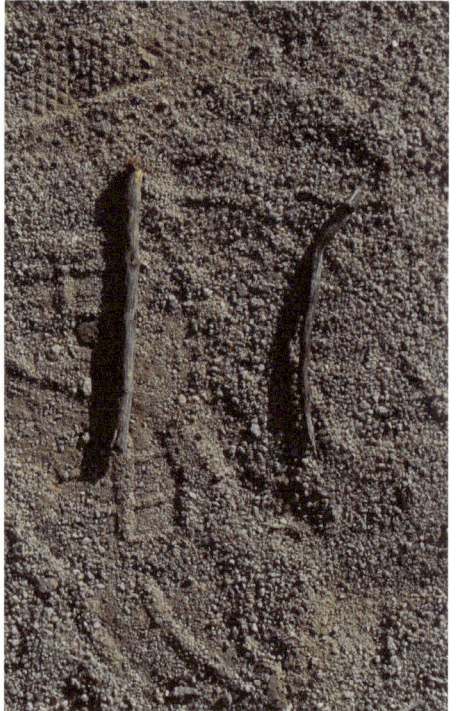
BONESTICK Date - ? Location - ?

Chapter 7 - Bonesticks

A BONESTICK is a stick that is so old it turned to a bone that's a stick but actually it's a bone. I have become so adept at finding BONESTICKS that I can quickly fill up several large trash bags with barely any effort. Then, it's off to my brother Ron's place to drop them off. Science can be frustrating work when Ron doesn't clean, organize and store my findings quickly. When that happens, my findings can pile up and block Ron's front door. He has no one to blame but himself and I am always careful to remind him of that.

BONESTICK Date - ? Location - ?

BONESTICK Date - ? Location - ?

BONESTICK Date - ? Location - ?

BONESTICK Date - ? Location - ?

BONESTICK Date - ? Location - ?

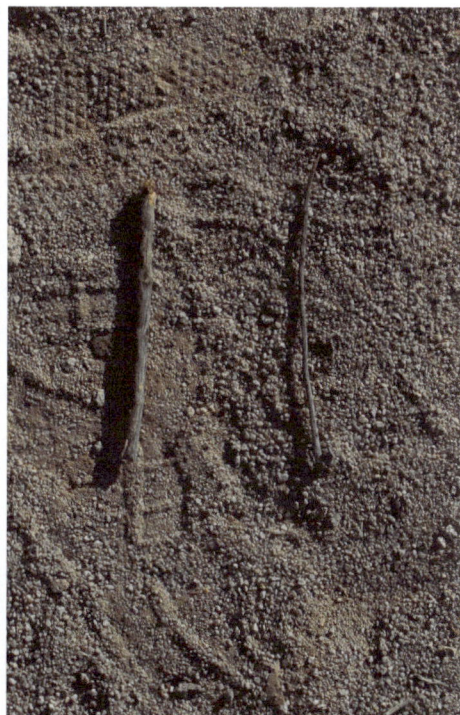
BONESTICK Date - ? Location - ?

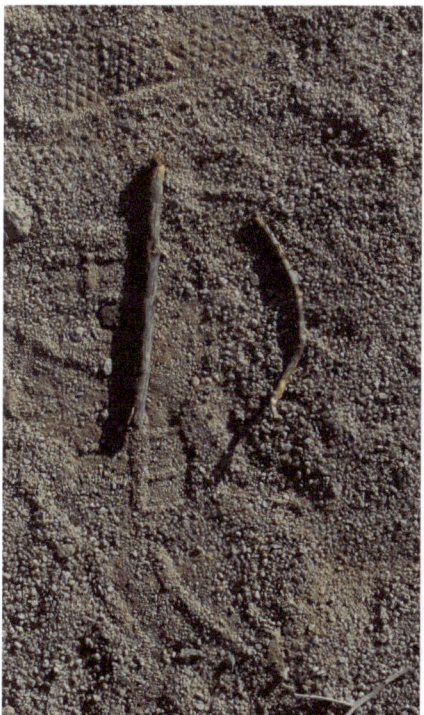
BONESTICK Date - ? Location - ?

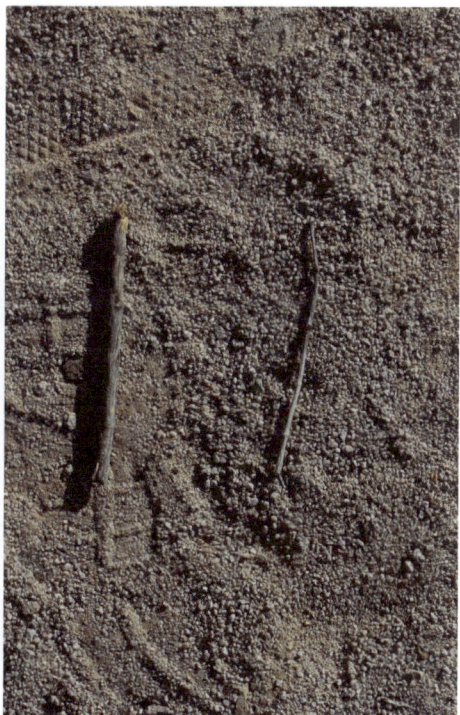
BONESTICK Date - ? Location - ?

21

BONESTICK Date - ? Location - ?

BONESTICK Date - ? Location - ?

BONESTICK Date - ? Location - ?

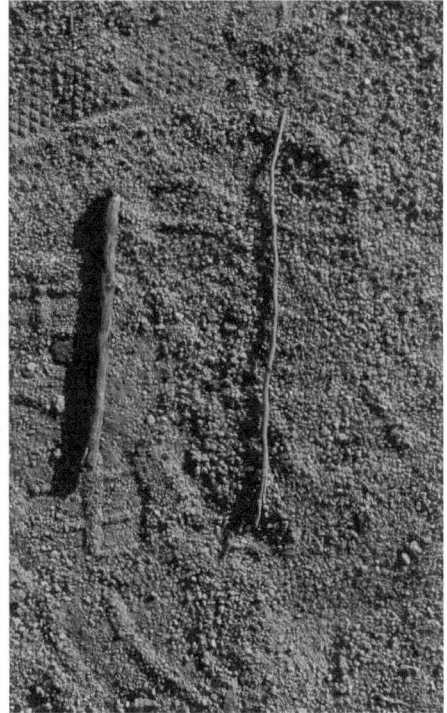
BONESTICK Date - ? Location - ?

BONESTICK Date - ? Location - ?

BONESTICK Date - ? Location - ?

BONESTICK Date - ? Location - ?

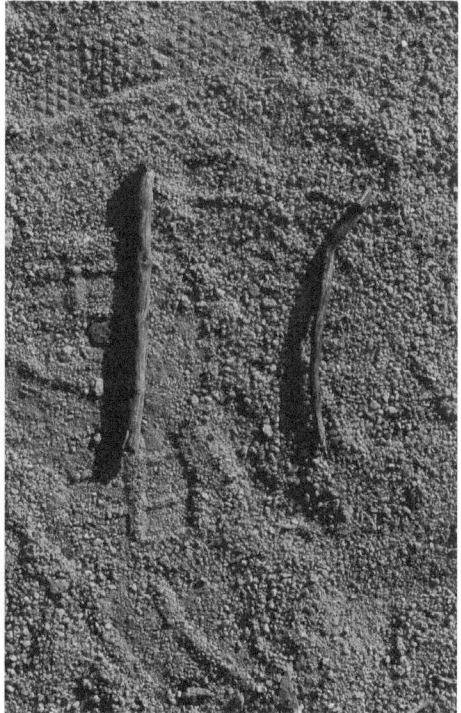
BONESTICK Date - ? Location - ?

23

BONESTICK Date - ? Location - ?

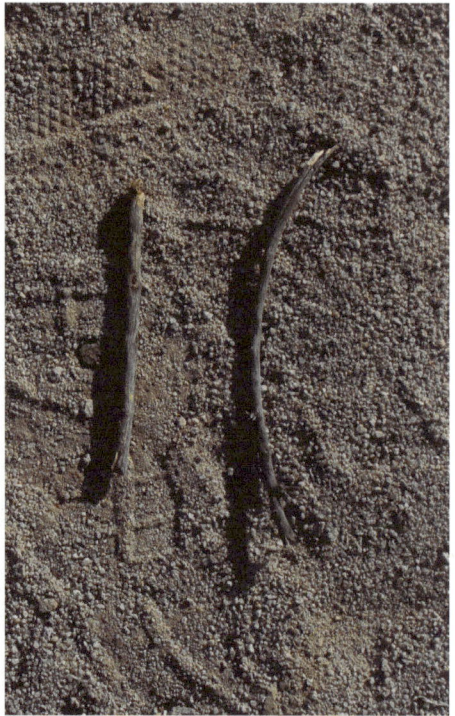
BONESTICK Date - ? Location - ?

BONESTICK Date - ? Location - ?

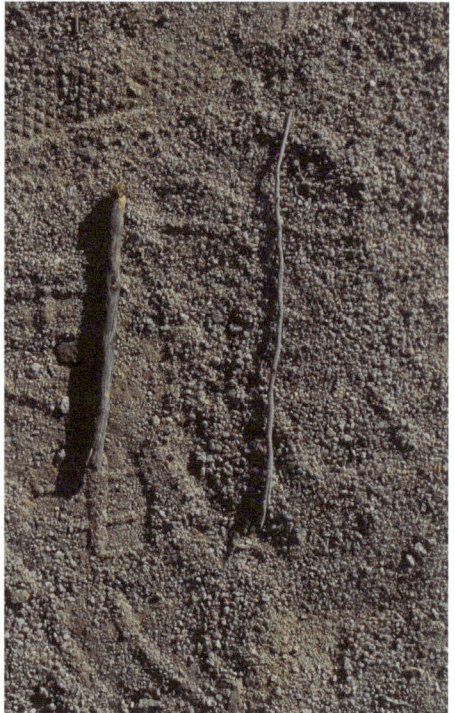
BONESTICK Date - ? Location - ?

BONESTICK Date - ? Location - ?

BONESTICK Date - ? Location - ?

BONESTICK Date - ? Location - ?

BONESTICK Date - ? Location - ?

BONESTICK Date - ? Location - ?

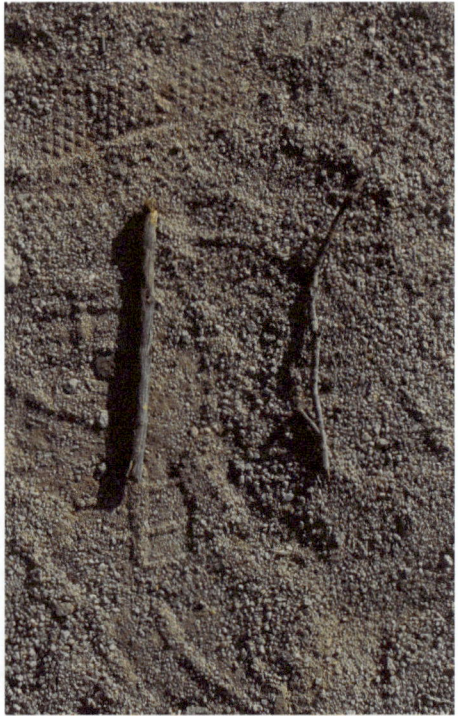
BONESTICK Date - ? Location - ?

BONESTICK Date - ? Location - ?

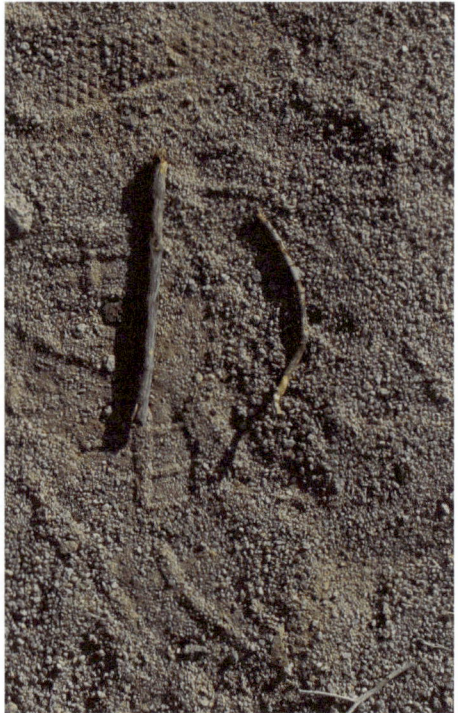
BONESTICK Date - ? Location - ?

BONESTICK Date - ? Location - ?

BONESTICK Date - ? Location - ?

BONESTICK Date - ? Location - ?

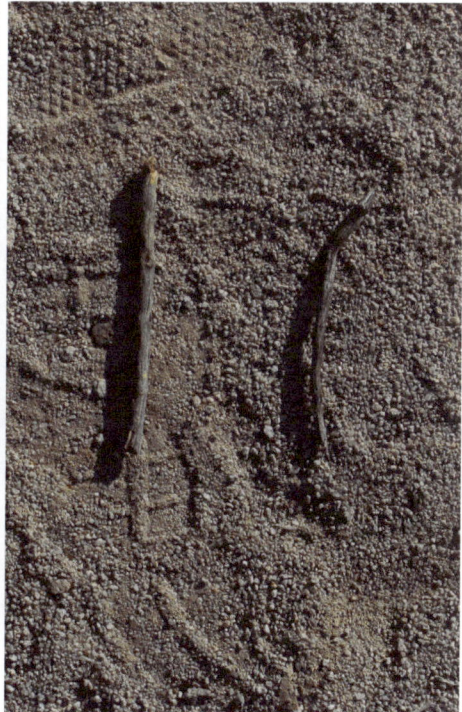

BONESTICK Date - ? Location - ?

Pointy Plant

Endangered Plant

Chapter 8 - Types of Plants

It has been said, that there is more than one type of plant. In my field work I have confirmed this to be true. But whether it is a NOCTUR-NAL PLANT, an AMPHIBIOUS PLANT or a POINTY PLANT, they all share certain qualities. For example, all plants are either STALAC-TITES, STALAGMITES or METEORITES. Knowing which is which requires a level of expertise unattainable to readers of this book. Also, some plants are ENDANGERED PLANTS. These plants are so endangered that they can cause you great harm. SAFE PLANTS are much better for people to do things with. ENDANGERED PLANTS should be destroyed so that they will finally stop hurting everyone.

Hole Plant

Unknown Type of Plant

Reference Rock

Small Rock   Date - ? Location - ?

Chapter 9 - Types of Rocks

There are many TYPES OF ROCKS. Some are small. Some are not as small. Some are round while others may be sort of oval shaped. Rocks were invented by the ANCIENT EGYPTIANS over a hundred years ago. No one spoke English back then. They only spoke CHINESE. When I find a rock, I put it in a cardboard box with all the other rocks. I am always careful to use a sturdy box that is not soggy because when I do, the box breaks and the rocks fall onto my brother Ron's foot. This may be funny to me but Ron has to go to the doctor. This of course keeps Ron from cleaning, sorting and storing MY FINDINGS in a timely manner. By staying healthy, Ron enables me to do the things I do.

Medium Sized Rock   Date - ? Location - ?

Medium Sized Rock   Date - ? Location - ?

Small Rock   Date - ? Location - ?

Very Small Rock   Date - ? Location - ?

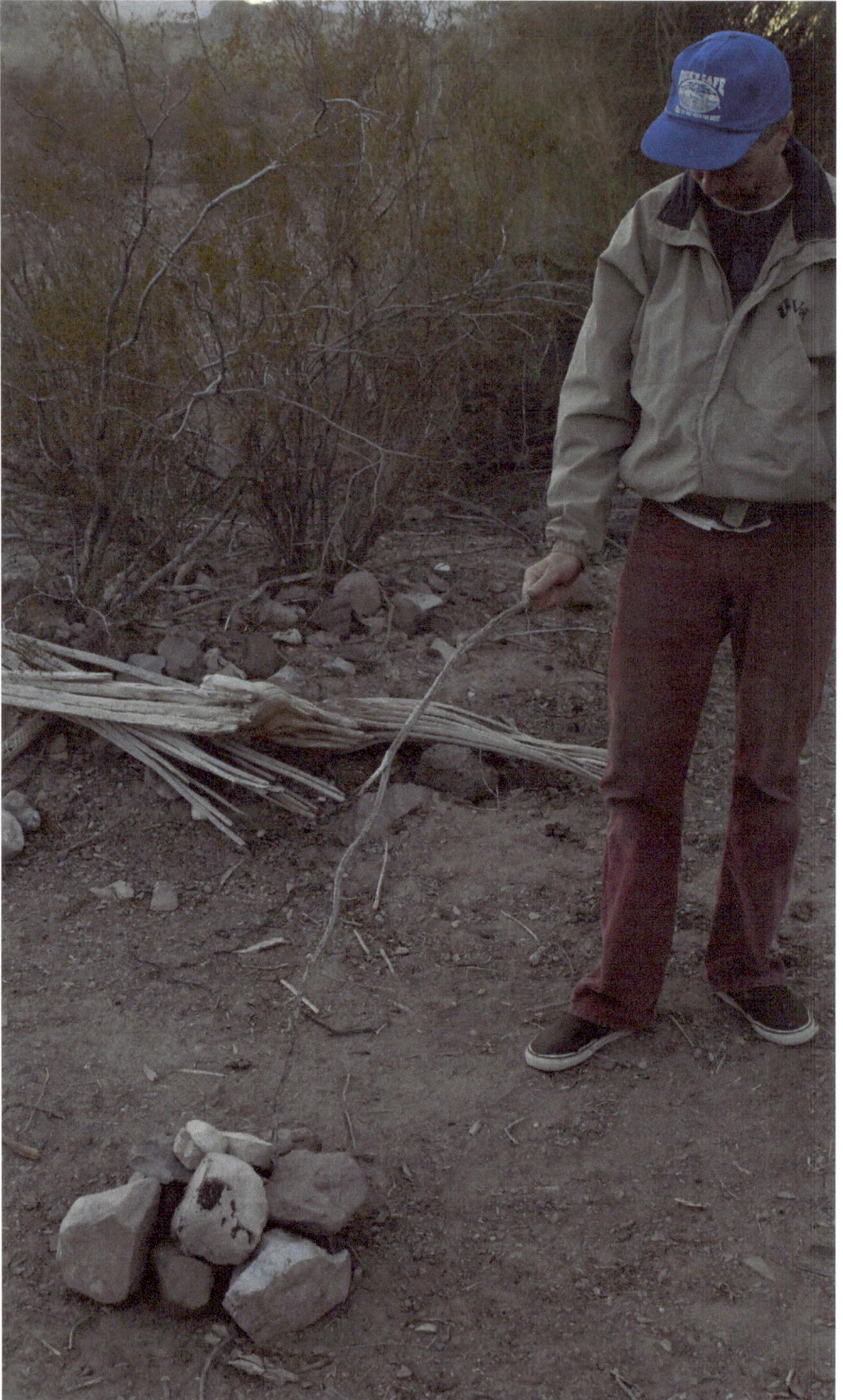

Chapter 10 - Mastodons

MASTODONS roamed this land over a hundred years ago. No one spoke english back then, they only spoke CHINESE. Mastodons are a type of dinosaur that laid their eggs in piles right on the ground where I can find them. Some of the eggs are medium sized. Others are small. These small eggs are the BABY MASTODON EGGS.

When I find a nest of MASTODON EGGS I become very excited because I know that this is a SIGNIFICANT FINDING. Anyone would be very impressed by the care and thoroughness with which I inspect a nest of MASTODON EGGS. There is no way to know what's hidden in a nest of MASTODON EGGS except to discover for myself!

36

Index

About the Author

Stu Cranstence has made a name for himself with an uncompromising dedication to his own special brand of unorthodox field work and his criticism of so-called "real scientists". He is a citizen scientist who spurns textbooks and the status quo and as a result he brings a fresh look to subjects that have often been overlooked in the annals of science literature. If you need to get a hold of him, you can find Stu "out in the field".

www.ingramcontent.com/pod-product-compliance
Lightning Source LLC
Chambersburg PA
CBHW040932030426
42336CB00001B/9